Loves illusions

Katie J. Woods , MS

Love's Illusions

"Finding The Courage To Let Go"

Written By:
Katie Woods
Illustrations By:
Gordon Kelley

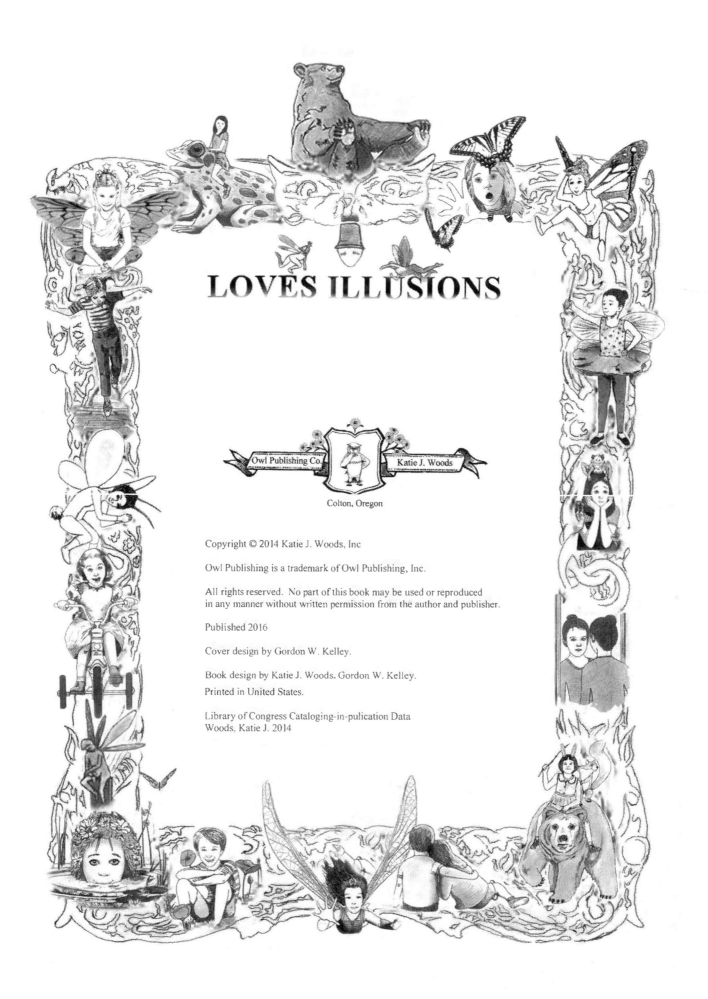

LOVES ILLUSIONS

Owl Publishing Co. — Katie J. Woods

Colton, Oregon

Published 2016

Cover design by Gordon W. Kelley.

Book design by Katie J. Woods. Gordon W. Kelley.
Printed in United States.

Library of Congress Cataloging-in-pulication Data
Woods, Katie J. 2014

Two amazing men continue to inspire me in my journey to help others by their words, encouragement, and genuine kindness.
With gratitude and thanksgiving I dedicate, "Loves Illusions," to Dr. John Green and Greg Crosby, two mentors who have taught me to replace the words, "I can't…with I can."

We are all searching for the "illusion of love," whether it be in a simple card, note, or thoughtful gesture. Too often we end up "at the other end of the stick," feeling hopelessly lost and unloved. The reality of what we hoped or dreamed of is often ignored, and we find ourselves in a dark tunnel reaching for a hand to guide us.

"Love's Illusions," is that hand…where you will find, hope and strength in a world in which the meaning of love has lost it's fervor…you will be guided through poem after poem in a heartfelt manner where dreams do come true and "Prince Charming" is still alive. I hope you will enjoy each page and the love I put into writing it…

When I was a little girl I was often beaten for no apparent reason. My stepfather was a Korean War Veteran who expected perfection. If the dishes weren't washed perfectly...if the floor wasn't swept to his satisfaction...if there was dust on the mantle...and I made any kind of excuse, I was punished severely. The harder I tried, the more I failed. I will never forget a particular day...I was trying to choke down collard greens, and he said I didn't appreciate his cooking. The next thing that I remember is him stuffing them down my throat while I was choking profusely. Days went into months, and I could not please him. I recall another occasion when my pollywog bowl was not cleaned to his standards. Before I could "fix" what he expected he put the garden hose in my mouth and preceded to drown me. I could recall countless stories, but the point that I am trying to make is that I could never please him "enough" nor "fix" the pain that caused him to be so cruel.

As the years passed I grew into a young woman...and you would think that I would choose a stable mate...not the case...all three of the mates that I chose were people that needed to be "fixed" and had similar characteristics to that of my step-dad. One of them beat me severely almost taking my life...another harmed my pets...and my last mate put my health in jeopardy several times.

Some of you that are reading these words are wondering what was wrong with the men that I tried to "help or fix." The big question is," what was wrong with me for giving them chance after chance when there was really no way that I could assist in their healing. All three of them had abusive fathers; all three of them had prior drinking or drug problems; and all three of them made me feel like a total failure. I was trying to "fix" my childhood but in doing so, I was destroying my life.

A few months ago I sought out a counselor, and he explained some simple premises. As children we are imprinted, and as we grow older we may seek the comfortableness of an abusing mate because it is what we are used to. This made total sense to me. For several years I had been seeking out someone with some of the characteristics of my stepfather.

Another premise that my therapist shared with me is that sometimes the vines of our childhood wrap around us choking the life out of us, and we have to be bold enough to get out the garden shears and begin to prune the vines that are literally "killing us." This may take some time, but with help, we can do it. And lastly, we can't be too hard on ourselves if we don't magically "prune our garden." It took time for us to develop unhealthy relationships, and it will take time for us to be whole again.

And here we are together reading, "Love's Illusions." It is about the journey that I have taken into "wholeness." Are all my branches gone? Almost...have a made some mistakes along the way? I sure have...but in doing so...I have grown into the woman that I want and need to share the rest of my life with. I know that you will find my book a comfort for any of you that have suffered from child or spousal abuse. Know that I love and care for each one of you who are reading these words. We are in this together...and WE WILL MAKE IT.

Flying
Above
Her

Sadness
Not
Wanting

To
Land
But

Hovering
So
Close

She
Could
Almost

Taste
The
Moistness

Of
Realistic
Sorrow

Once
I
Wished

Upon
A
Star

Hoping
For
Childhood

Magic
And
Believing

In
Fairy
Tales

Today
I
Realized

That
The
Tooth

Fairy
Doesn't
Exist

And
Wishes
Never

Do
Come
True…or do they?

Ghosted…unable to breathe
Unable to think…
Unable to feel…
Locked in a box…
Nails pounding…
Suffocating…no breath.

Ghosted…never heard…
Spoke about…
No feelings…no thoughts…
Smothering…
In the words…
That were never said.

Set
Up
To

Fail
Time
And

Time
Again
Wondering

What
I
Did

Wrong
To
Deserve

This
Disclusion
Of

Unimaginable
Pain
That

No-one
Understands
Anyway…

Carrying
Lost
Dreams

In
A
Basket

So
Full
She

Could
Only
Imagine

How
To
Replace

Her
Sadness
With

A
Heart
Full of love..

Sometimes their are turns in life that seem unbearable and then amazingly enough we come to a path showing a sign with our name on it...and we know without a doubt...we need to take our compass out and change direction. Thank you God for always listening through the years and giving yourself to help me make some new decisions in my life. You are an amazing God and I know you are watching over me...as I write these thoughts. Take them...and heal my broken heart.

I wish
I wish I could turn
Back time…

No trip…
No sickness
No forbidden visit

To
The
Un-visitable…

I wish
That
Life

Had
Stopped
Seven

Days
Ago…
And

The
Heart wrenching
Pain

I
Am
Feeling now…

WOULD LEAVE FOREVER

In the essence
 of the moment
 her heart froze

 and she felt nothingness
 …a void so empty
 in a chasm of despair

 …pain…anguish…lost…
as she held him in her
arms

nothingness overcame her
and words
   were vacant as her tears fell

…in a torrent of passionless grief…

Looking
Back
At

The
Pain
And

Sadness
Wishing
It

Had
Been
Different

Or
Maybe
I

Had
Been
And

Yet
It
Would

Have
Turned
Out

The
Same
Or would it?

In
The
Event

Of...
A
Miracle

Hang
On
Tight

And
Dance
Your

Way
Through
It

Knowing
That
You

Are
Blessed
By

All
The
Love

God
Could
Possibly give you...

Amidst
The
Stillness

Of
Night
Our

Souls
Yearn
For

Childhood
Dreams
And

Magical
Fairytale
Moments…

Reach
Out
Dear

Caterpillars
The
Butterflies

Are
Waiting
To

Guide
You
Through

The
Heavenly
Universe…

Friendship…
The illusive magic
That you need and feel
Is here…when you are ready…

Waiting
Patiently
Knowing the heartfelt
Dream

Walking
At twilight
Not alone
Hand and hand

Outermost deserts
Transformed
Into rivers
Always as one…

In
The
Magic

Of
The
Moment

A
Tear
Fell

Not
Of
Sadness

But
Joy
Knowing

That
She
Had

Somehow
Made
It

And
Finally
Was

Truly
Loved
By

Not
One
But

All
The
Stars

In
The
Universe

Emmeshed
In
Your heart

Is
A
Place

You
Can
Only find

A secret place
Filled
With

Magic
For
Safekeeping

With
Silver
Wings

She
Soared
Embracing

Galaxies
Of
Stars

Repeating
Her
Heart song…

Each
Night
She

Searched
For
Him

In
Her
Dreams

Often
Finding
Him

Sitting
In
The

Poppy
Field
With

A
Smile
On

His
Face
And

A
Child-like
Grin

Life is a beautiful dance...

And...sometimes it's hard...

To take the first step...

Should I?

Could I?

Would I?

Want to reach out...

Make the first move...

Knowing...not knowing?

Is it right or wrong?

But taking the risk

Anyway...

Realizing it is better

That I dance...

Than standing on the sidelines of life...

Prince
Charming
Arrived

Fully
Clothed
And

Decked
Out
Wearing

A
Black
Jacket

Instead
Of
A

White
Coat
And

Carrying
One
Daisy

Instead
Of
A Dozen Roses

Under the street

 Lamp

The fairies played

At midnight

Sorting out

Wishes

Sprinkling

Dust

Amidst

The requests

Of

Children

Kept in a box…
Unable to breathe…
Unable to feel…
Unable to reason…
Unable to find a way out…

Come sweet dream
And
Carry me over the rainbow…
Where children play
And frolic in the wind…

Where fairy tales come true
And magic butterflies carry me to the sunshine…
Where I am allowed to breathe
And feel and reason…
And finally…Find a way back home…

Enchanted
Moments
And

Mystical
Illusions
Of

Past
Desires
Found

In
The
Translations

Of
Fairytale
Magic

And
Filled
With

The
Imagination
Of the heart...

Sometimes
in
 the

middle
of
 life's storms

 a peace
envelops
you...

when your
brain
simultaneously

connects
to your body
and a
.
freedom
simply says
..."yesssssssss."

Lilies blowing
In the wind
Gently
Calling

Walk
With me
Gentle Breezes
Carry me home

Orange and yellow
Bobbing heads
Seemingly real
Yet silent

Take my hand
Tightly
Finger tips
Letting go

Moments
Where
Memories

Are
So
Close

You
Can
Reach

Out
And
Touch

Them
Even
Though

They
Are
Just

Voices
In
The wind...

Love Is Fragile
Like The Wings Of A Butterfly...
Delicate...

Oh Dear One...
Put Me In A Glass Case
And Nurture Me

For My Wings Are Wet
And Have Forgotten
How To Fly

I
Felt
Your

Breath
Against
My

Brow
Just
For

A
Millisecond
When you

Were
Letting
Me

Know
That
You

Were
Close
Remembering…

Just
As
I

Was
In
Our

Magical
Moment
That

Only
We
Felt…

The wind
Swept
Her away

Carrying her
To
The Heavens

Wings
Encompassed
Her

Saving
Her dreams
For safekeeping

Each
Night
She

Walked
In
Her

Dreams
Finding
The

Unmarked
Path
Where

The
Moon
Cast

A
Shadow
On

The
Glistening
Raindrops

Helping
Her
Find Her Way...

In the midst of sadness
A tear falls
Waiting to be caught
By A passer by...
Knowing in that moment
Hearts intertwine
And there is an understanding
That doesn't
Need any explanation
THIS IS LOVE...

His
Eyes
Caught

Mine
And
In

An
Instant
I

Knew
Just
Knew

Unconditional
Love
Without

Reservation
No
Words

Just
Feelings
That

One
And
One

Didn't
Equal
Two...

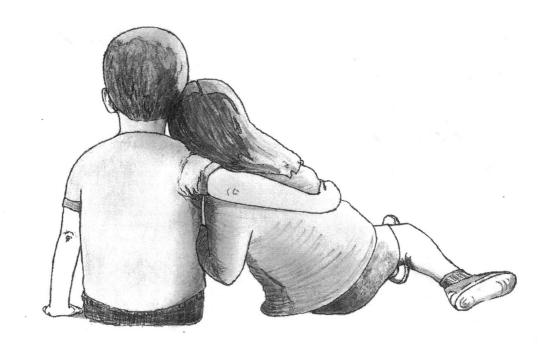

In
A
Single

Moment
Of
Time

Her
Heart
Changed

From
Lost
To

Found
And
In

That
Millisecond
She

Knew
That
She

Would
Never
Be Lost Again…

Untie
Yours
Strings

For
The
Last

Time
Knowing
This

Is
What
God

Has
Given
You

His
Beautiful
Gift

Free
And
With

No
Conditions
Wrapped

Up
In
HIS PACKAGE…

ONCE upon a time there was a little girl who lived in the forest. Every day she would try as hard as she could to please her Papa, but every night she cried herself to sleep knowing that she had failed again.

One day she decided to make a list of everything that she did in hopes that she could improve herself.

1. Get up with Papa and make his lunch

2. Lay out Papa's breakfast

3. Make Papa's dinner

4. Warm Papa's bathroom, so he can enjoy his shower

5. Lay out Papa's evening clothes

6. Encourage Papa whenever he hurts

7. Give Papa his pills

8. Fetch things for Papa when he forgets

9. Complete Papa's important paperwork.

After completing her list, the little girl realized that she had to come up with one more thing, so she would make it an even 10. She thought and thought, but nothing came to her mind.

Days passed and the little girl continued to try. At times her Papa would seem pleased with her; at others he would growl at her, and the little girl would feel heart broken..

One day the little girl got sick and as hard as she tried she could not get well. Tears fell like waterfalls, and she didn't know what to do.. As hard as she tried to tell

Papa that he had to be soft, he would growl about 75% of the time, and during these times, the little girl would give up.

After what seemed an eternity, the little girl became sicker and sicker, and in desperation, she decided to run away from home. She walked and walked in the forest, and finally met an ugly green frog. His voice was soft…and he looked at her with kindness. Day after day they played, and slowly the little girl got well.

Years passed, and the little girl grew more and more attached to the ugly green frog. She told her Papa about him, and he stood up tall and really GROWLED…the little girl looked at him, and somehow she wasn't sad anymore, because she had found a friend to love.

One day the little girl and the ugly green frog ran away together and were never seen again…because we all know that frogs do turn into princes when they are loved.

And isn't that what life is all about, "loving one another, and showing it." And that…would have been number 10 on the little girl's list.

Made in United States
Orlando, FL
24 June 2022